Mommy, The Rush Rush People are Coming!
Part 1

Child Sensitive Reality Series

by Mickey Moondust

Little seven year old Anastasiya
stops playing suddenly
as she hears an unfamiliar sound
coming over the nearby hill.

She stands to her feet while tightly holding onto her soft handmade bunny. A tank is coming over the hill.

Anastasiya dashes for the front door as a second tank comes over the hill. Now there are a few soldiers as well.

Anastasiya yells, "Mommy! Daddy! The Rush Rush people are coming!"

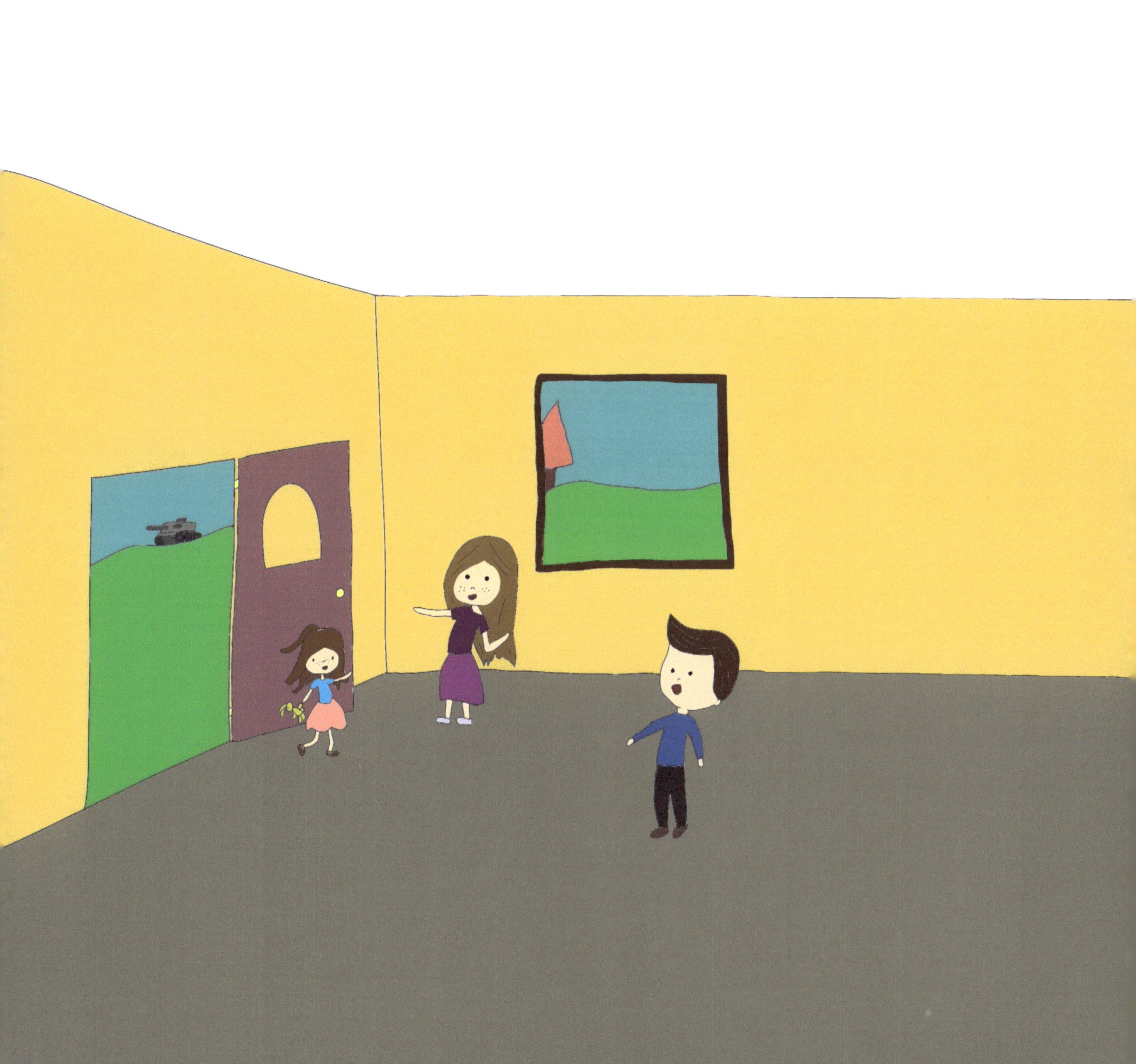

Mom and dad are surprised for a moment
as they look out of the window to see.

"We need to hurry!" mom said.
Dad darts around grabbing some clothes and food while stuffing a backpack.

BOOM! CRASH! The neighbors' house is broken now. It is good that the neighbors' were not home.

"Why?" asks Anastasiya,
"I don't get it."
She picks up another of her
favorite toys.
It is a soft tiny handmade doll.

"Come, come!" mom says, as she hastens Anastasiya to the back door.

Now outside against the back of the house, dad peers around the corner cautiously to see where the soldiers are.

OOPS! He is seen!

"Come out NOW!" the soldier shouts.

Dad grabs Anastasiya's and mom's hands and runs into the nearby woods.

With a smile of encouragement, mom looks into Anastasiya's eyes and says, "It is almost dark, we will be just fine... and we are all together!"

Anastasiya smiles cheerfully and says,
"Yay, my bunny and doll
will be safe too."

So, Anastasiya and her parents vanish deeper into the woods escaping the Rush Rush people.

To be continued...

Join us in the next part of this
child sensitive reality series:

Mommy, The Rush Rush People are Coming
Part 2

www.ingramcontent.com/pod-product-compliance
Lightning Source LLC
LaVergne TN
LVHW071221160826
845679LV00003B/890
9798366562218